all you need to know

CW01662946

FOSTERING REGULATIONS, GUIDANCE & NMS England

The Fostering Network

www.fostering.net

First edition published by The Fostering Network 2011
Second edition published 2015

3 5 7 9 10 8 6 4 2

Printed and bound by
Partridges, Northampton

Text
Doug Lawson

Design
Johnny Burke

A CIP catalogue record for this book is available from the British Library

ISBN 1 897869 62 2

Introduction

Through policy and legislation, successive governments have continued to afford a high priority to ensuring that vulnerable children who are in the care of the local authorities receive all the protection, help and support they need to do well in life. At the heart of this the message is loud and clear: foster carers must be treated as core members of the team around the child, with the recognition and respect they deserve and the support they need.

Foster carers can expect to be fully involved in care planning, and to be given the authority to make day-to-day decisions about the children in their care. At times, though, the raft of regulations, government guidance and national minimum standards can seem a little overwhelming – not just to foster carers but also to social workers and others who work with children in care.

The Fostering Network has produced this guide to cut through the jargon and complexities of legislation, to help to make sure that every foster carer can be sure that they are being given appropriate support to meet the needs of some of our most vulnerable children.

About the author

Doug Lawson is an independent children's services consultant, trainer and researcher who works with a wide range of fostering services, local authorities and voluntary organisations. He was engaged by the Department for Education to work on the 2011 review of the Children Act 1989 guidance, drafting the revised statutory guidance on fostering services and on family and friends care. He also contributed to guidance on transitions to adulthood for care leavers and on children's homes.

Prior to his current role Doug had substantial experience of strategic, policy and operational leadership of children's social care services in local authorities, including responsibility for fostering services. He also led the fostering workstream of the government's Looked After Children Taskforce, helping local authorities to improve delivery of fostering services and commissioning of placements for looked after children.

Doug is author of other titles in The Fostering Network's acclaimed *All You Need to Know* series, including *Family and Friends Foster Care; A Foster Care Handbook for Supervising Social Workers;* and *Planning for Looked After Children: A Handbook for Children's Social Workers.*

Contents

How to use this guide

This guide is for everyone concerned with foster care in England – including foster carers, social workers in both care planning and fostering services, members of fostering panels, independent reviewing officers and managers with responsibility for looked after children. It has been written specially to help you to understand the legal framework that governs fostering services. It includes practice guidance to help you to implement the changes effectively, and spells out the roles of different people and how they can best work together as a team.

Where they are referred to in the text you will find references (in italics) down the side of each page to the various standards, regulations and statutory guidance which have to be met, so that you can follow these up in more detail. All of the documents referred to are available from the government website **www.gov.uk** or from The Fostering Network at **www.fostering.net**. Unless stated otherwise, references to 'regulations' mean the Fostering Services (England) Regulations 2011 (as amended), and references to 'guidance' mean the Children Act 1989 Guidance and Regulations Volume 4: Fostering Services. References to 'standards' mean the Fostering Services National Minimum Standards.

There are also some questions at the end of each section to help you to think about how well these requirements are being met in your own experience.

Each section of the guide has been colour coded so that you can easily find the information you are looking for, but to make sure you don't miss anything important you will find it best to read it through first of all.

Foster carers work as part of a team, so this guide takes account of what social workers and others need to do in partnership with foster carers to meet the needs of children and young people.

There is a glossary of terms on page 78.

1) The legal framework

Fostering services can be provided by fostering agencies (often known as independent fostering providers or IFPs) and by local authorities. Legally, they are collectively known as 'fostering service providers' but for simplicity this guide refers to them as 'fostering services'. They all have to comply with requirements set by the Children Act 1989 and the Care Standards Act 2000, and regulations made under those Acts, as well as National Minimum Standards (usually known as NMS).

The relationship between these and the way in which they apply to fostering services is explained in the following table.

Regulations, Guidance and National Minimum Standards

	Purpose	Most directly relevant to fostering services
Regulations	Regulations are legislation in the same way as acts of parliament, and **must** always be complied with by everyone concerned.	The Fostering Services (England) Regulations 2011
Statutory Guidance	Issued by government and explains what local authorities **must** do, as well as complying with acts of parliament and regulations, when they are delivering services or buying them from other organisations.	Children Act 1989 Guidance and Regulations Volume 4: Fostering Services (2011)
National Minimum Standards (NMS)	Describe the **absolute minimum standards** that the government requires of organisations delivering services. Used by inspectors to judge the quality of services and whether or not these comply with regulations. Also useful for carrying out self-assessments of services, as a basis for induction, and to guide staff and foster carers through their work.	Fostering Services: National Minimum Standards (2011)

The regulations, guidance and NMS relevant to fostering services were all revised in 2011 to make them clearer and more streamlined, and to provide greater flexibility to exercise professional judgement. This guide should help staff and foster carers to exercise their professional judgement, but for greater detail regarding the framework for working with looked after children reference should always be made to the documents themselves.

For each of the standards in the new NMS there is a related outcome to be achieved by the fostering service. The outcomes are designed to focus on the needs of children, and to be measurable. As long as the regulations are complied with there is no need to follow every standard exactly, so long as it can be shown that the outcome is still being met. The standards also show how they relate to the underpinning legislation.

General introduction to the NMS

The regulations, statutory guidance and NMS are not just relevant to staff of fostering services: it is essential that everyone who works with children and young people in foster care is aware of what they say. There are other regulations and statutory guidance which also impact on fostering services, particularly those relating to care planning. These are sometimes amended or supplemented so it's important to always refer to the latest version. The most relevant are summarised in the following table.

Legislation and guidance most relevant to fostering services

Assessment and Approval of foster Carers: Amendments to the Children Act 1989 Guidance and Regulations	(July 2013) Revised statutory guidance on assessment and approval.
Care Leavers (England) Regulations 2010	Designed to ensure that young people leaving care receive the same support that would be expected of any reasonable parent.
Care Planning, Placement and Case Review (England) Regulations 2010	Specify requirements for care plans and placement plans, placement decisions, monitoring and review of looked after children. Amended in 2013 and 2014.

Legislation and guidance most relevant to fostering services *contd.*

Care Planning, Placement and Case Review and Fostering Services (Miscellaneous Amendments) Regulations 2013	Amend the relevant regulations with regard to the assessment and approval of foster carers and delegation of authority.
Care Standards Act 2000	Sets the regulatory and inspectoral regime for children's homes and fostering services and establishes National Minimum Standards.
Children Act 1989	The primary legislation governing looked after children, children's homes and fostering services.
Children Act 1989 Guidance and Regulations Volume 2: Care Planning, Placement and Case Review	(2010) Provides a central reference point for local authority work with looked after children. Amended July 2013 with regard to delegation of authority and February 2014 with regard to contact with siblings. Supplemented April 2014 concerning looked after children and youth justice and July 2014 in relation to out of authority placements.
Children Act 1989 Guidance and Regulations Volume 3: Planning Transition to Adulthood for Care Leavers	(Revised May 2014 and January 2015) Statutory guidance on how to meet the requirements of the Care Leavers (England) Regulations 2010, updated to include staying put duties and more information on suitable accommodation.
Children Act 1989 Guidance and Regulations Volume 4: Fostering Services	(2011) Contains the requirements set out by government to support local authorities, working with fostering service providers, in giving the best possible care and support to children in foster care. Amended July 2013 with regard to assessment and approval of foster carers and delegation of authority.
Children and Young Persons Act 2008	The primary legislation governing services for care leavers.
The Children's Homes and Looked After Children (Miscellaneous Amendments) (England) Regulations 2013	Amend the Fostering Services (England) Regulations 2011 by requiring fostering services to agree with the police a policy regarding children who go missing, and substituting 'sexual exploitation' for 'prostitution' in schedule 7.

Legislation and guidance most relevant to fostering services *contd.*

Delegation of Authority to Carers: Amendments to the Children Act 1989 Guidance and Regulations	(July 2013) Amends the fostering guidance and care planning guidance.
Delegation of Authority to Carers – Developing your local policy	(March 2014) Non-statutory guidance.
Delegation of Authority to Carers	Young people's guide (April 2014).
Early Permanence Placements and Approval of Prospective Adopters as Foster carers – Statutory Guidance for Local Authorities and Adoption Agencies	(July 2014) Statutory guidance on fostering for adoption.
Family and Friends Care: Statutory Guidance for Local Authorities	(2011) Sets out a framework for the provision of support to family and friends carers, including the assessment and support of family and friends foster carers.
Fostering Services (England) Regulations 2011	Regulate all fostering services. Amended July 2013 and April 2014.
Fostering Services: National Minimum Standards	(2011) Set the minimum standards required of all fostering services.
IRO Handbook: Statutory Guidance for Independent Reviewing Officers and Local Authorities on their Functions in Relation to Case Management and Review for Looked After Children	(2010) Guides independent reviewing officers in the discharge of their responsibilities towards looked after children, with the aim that they receive the support and services required to meet their full potential.
Junior Individual Saving Accounts for Looked After Children: statutory guidance for local authorities	(2012)

Looked After Children: Contact with Siblings - update to The Children Act 1989 Guidance and Regulations Volume 2: Care Planning, Placement and Case Review	(February 2014) Supersedes the relevant section of volume 2 as originally published.
Out of Authority Placement of Looked After Children: Supplement to The Children Act 1989 Volume 2: Care Planning, Placement and Case Review Guidance (July 2014	Statutory guidance relating to amendments to the Care Planning, Placement and Case Review (England) Regulations 2010 which created new requirements for local authorities making 'distant' placements.
Promoting the Education of Looked After Children – Statutory guidance for local authorities	(July 2014) Replaces 2010 version.
Short Breaks: Statutory Guidance on how to Safeguard and promote the Welfare of Disabled Children using Short Breaks	(2010) Seeks to improve outcomes for disabled children through short breaks provision.
Statutory Guidance on Children Who Run Away or go Missing from Home or Care	(Revised January 2014). There is also a separate flowchart showing roles and responsibilities when a child goes missing from care.
Statutory Guidance on Promoting the Health and Well-being of Looked After Children	Statutory guidance from 2009 (under review).
Working Together to Safeguard Children	(Revised 2013) Statutory guidance on how organisations and individuals should work together to safeguard and promote the welfare of children.

Things to think about: the legal framework

	yes	no
Do you understand the difference in purpose of the relevant regulations, national minimum standards and statutory guidance?	☐	☐
Do you have access to these documents when you need to refer to them?	☐	☐

2) Supporting the fostering task

The role of foster carers

The government has made it clear through the statutory guidance that foster carers have a challenging and key role in caring for vulnerable children, which requires skill, knowledge, expertise, self-awareness, commitment and the ability to work as part of a team. To undertake this role successfully it is seen as essential that their contribution to improving outcomes for looked after children is appropriately recognised and acknowledged, their status respected and their levels of authority clearly defined so that they can give children in their care a full experience of family life, safeguard them and help them to grow and realise their potential.

Guidance 2.4

Values underpinning foster care

The NMS are based on an important set of principles that should influence all of the work of foster carers and those who work with them. They make it clear that foster carers cannot do their job properly without appropriate support from social workers and others.

The principles are contained in the following value statement:

- The child's welfare, safety and needs are at the centre of their care.
- Children should have an enjoyable childhood, and benefit from excellent parenting and education, enjoying a wide range of opportunities to develop their talents and skills leading to a successful adult life.
- Children are entitled to grow up in a loving environment that can meet their developmental needs.
- Every child should have his or her wishes and feelings listened to and taken into account.
- Each child should be valued as an individual and given personalised support in line with their individual needs and background in order to develop their identity, self-confidence and self-worth.
- The particular needs of disabled children and children with complex needs will be fully recognised and taken into account.
- The significance of contact for looked after children, and of maintaining relationships with birth parents and the wider family, including siblings, half-siblings and grandparents, is recognised, as is the foster carer's role in this.
- Children in foster care deserve to be treated as a good parent would treat their own children and to have the opportunity for as full an experience of family life and childhood as possible, without unnecessary restrictions.
- The importance of the child's relationship with their foster carer should be acknowledged and foster carers should be recognised as core members of the team working with the child.
- Foster carers have a right to full information about the child.
- It is essential that foster carers receive relevant support services and development opportunities in order to provide the best care for children.
- Genuine partnership between all those involved in fostering children is essential for the NMS to deliver the best outcomes for children; this includes the government, local government, other statutory agencies, fostering service providers and foster carers.

Supervision and support of foster carers

Regulation 17
Standard 21

Foster carers must receive the support and supervision they need in order to care properly for the children placed with them. The NMS emphasise that foster carers must have access to proper support from social workers and other professionals, as well as information and advice including assistance to deal with other services such as health and education. Foster carers may also need appropriate breaks from caring to enable them to continue to meet children's needs.

Child's social worker

The child's social worker is responsible for the child's care plan and should:

- Make sure that the foster carer has all the information they need to care for the child.
- Ensure that a placement plan is agreed with the foster carer.
- Provide advice, guidance and assistance to help the foster carer to meet the child's needs in accordance with their care plan.

Supervising social worker

The supervising social worker is responsible for supervising and supporting the foster carer, including:

- Making regular visits, including at least one unannounced visit a year.
- Supervising the foster carer's work to ensure that they are meeting the child's needs.
- Providing emotional and practical support.
- Assessing the foster carer's performance and supporting their skills development.

Fostering service

The fostering service should:

- Provide the foster carer with information about the regulations, standards, guidance, policies and procedures within which they need to work, including information about investigating allegations, financial support, and insurance.
- Have a policy setting out how it supports foster carers.
- Provide out-of-hours support to foster carers.
- Support the sons and daughters of foster carers and other members of the household.
- Provide support groups and support foster care associations and peer mentoring.
- Provide training and support for foster carers to maintain a development portfolio, including evidencing the national *Training, Support and Development Standards for Foster Care.*
- Provide clear information about fostering allowances, ensuring that these cover the full cost of caring for children placed, and review them annually in consultation with foster carers.
- Apply allowances and fees consistently and fairly to all foster carers who meet the criteria, including family and friends foster carers.

Financial support

Standard 28 Guidance 5.71-5.73

Foster carers have to be supplied every year with the fostering service's policy about payments, so they are clear about the fees, allowances and expenses they will receive. These have to be reviewed annually and foster carers consulted in advance of any changes made. Allowances paid must be at least the national minimum level set by the Department for Education, plus any agreed necessary additional expenses so that the full cost of caring for the child is reimbursed.

Standard 28

The payment policy should include information about what allowances and fees are paid during a break in placement or an investigation into an allegation.

There is no obligation to pay foster carers a fee as well as an allowance, but where fees are paid the criteria cannot discriminate against any particular groups of foster carers and must be open to all who meet the criteria.

An annual statement of the payments made to each foster carer has to be provided at the end of each tax year.

Learning and development

Standard 20

Foster carers must keep a training and development portfolio which shows how they meet the skills they require to foster. They must each evidence that they meet the relevant Training Support and Development Standards set by the Department for Education within the set timescales. There are various workbooks and guidance to support this available from the government website www.gov.uk/government/collections/guidance-for-foster-carers . Supervising social workers and others within the fostering service must provide support and training to help foster carers to achieve the necessary standards which will enable them to meet the needs of their fostered children. This must include safer caring.

The Fostering Network publishes *Safer Caring: a new approach* in its *Pathways Through Fostering* series – for information visit **www.fostering resources.co.uk**

Things to think about: supporting foster carers

Children's social workers and supervising social workers

	yes	no
Are foster carers fully recognised as core members of the team?	☐	☐
Are the sons and daughters of foster carers supported as part of the fostering household?	☐	☐
Do children's social workers engage foster carers when they visit, and offer appropriate advice and support?	☐	☐
Is there effective communication between supervising social workers and children's social workers?	☐	☐

Fostering services

	yes	no
Do all foster carers have an allocated supervising social worker?	☐	☐
Is relevant advice and support available outside office hours?	☐	☐
Are appropriate breaks from caring provided, taking account of children's needs?	☐	☐
Is there a comprehensive and accessible training programme for foster carers?	☐	☐
Is there a clear policy about allowances and fees, and are foster carers consulted when this is reviewed annually?	☐	☐
Does the financial support policy discriminate against any groups of foster carers?	☐	☐

Foster carers

	yes	no
Do you receive adequate social work and other professional support, information and advice?	☐	☐
Are you helped to understand the regulations, standards, policies and procedures relevant to your role?	☐	☐
Are you always involved in reviews and other meetings about the children you foster?	☐	☐
Are you clear about the financial and other support available to you?	☐	☐

3) Making and ending foster placements

Matching

Guidance 3.1-3.8
Standards 11 and 15

Children should be matched with an appropriate foster carer capable of meeting their needs. They should feel welcomed into the foster home, treated and valued as a member of the family, and included in the everyday life of the family. They should, in due course, leave a placement in a planned and sensitive manner which makes them feel valued.

Children Act 1989 s.22c

Care Planning Placement and Case Review (England) Regulations 2010 regulation 22(3)(b)

The law requires that when making a specific foster placement the social worker must be satisfied that fostering is the best way to meet their duties towards the child, and that it is the most appropriate placement in the circumstances. If there are already any children placed with the foster carer then the consent of their social workers has to be obtained before making the new placement. The purpose of this is to consider if it is suitable for all the children to be placed in the same household, and whether the foster carer may need any additional support to meet all of their needs. Standard 15.1 makes it clear that a placement should not be proposed unless it can be reasonably expected to meet the child's assessed needs, and the impact on other children has been considered. The fostering service should keep a record of the decision making process. Every effort should be made to place brothers and sisters in the same foster home, providing this is consistent with their needs.

In an emergency a child can be placed with a foster carer outside of their terms of approval, but for a maximum of six working days. This is only allowed exceptionally, in unforeseen circumstances, and not as an alternative to making appropriate contingency plans. The care planning guidance makes clear that:

Children Act 1989 Guidance and Regulations Volume 2: Care Planning Placement and Case Review, 3.85

> *Foster carer assessments are designed to identify the ages, number or needs of the children to whom the foster carer is most likely to offer the best care. Research evidence consistently shows that placement outside the terms of approval are significantly more likely to result in placement breakdown, often if there is already a fostered child in the household.*

Care Planning Placement and Case Review (England) Regulations 2010 regulation 11; Children Act 1989 Guidance and Regulations Volume 2: Care Planning, Placement and Case Review 3.28-3.40

The child must always be moved to a more appropriate placement within six working days, unless the foster carer's terms of approval have been changed in the meantime.

A child cannot be placed with a foster carer who lives outside the boundary of the local authority without the permission of a named senior officer who has been given the power to consent to these placements. This does not apply if the foster carer is approved by the same local authority, even though they live outside its area, or the foster carer is a 'connected person' (see page 64) to the child.

Information needed by foster carers

Regulation 17
Standard 15
Guidance 3.6
Children Act 1989 Guidance and Regulations Volume 2: Care Planning, Placement and Case Review 3.134

Foster carers must be given all the information that they need about the child to enable them to care for them properly and this must be kept up to date as necessary. This always includes the care plan and the placement plan, as explained in sections 4 and 5 of this guide. It is the responsibility of the child's social worker to make sure that this information is available for the foster carer, but the fostering service is responsible for following this up if the social worker fails to do so.

The information needed by foster carers has to be provided before the placement is made, although it is accepted that when an emergency placement is made it may have to be given at the time of the placement. There may be exceptional circumstances (perhaps when a child is placed in an emergency arising out of hours) when the fostering service does not have all of the information, even at the time of placement; in a case like this, it must be provided as soon as possible – and within five working days.

Ending placements

Standard 15.3
Guidance 3.5

Once a child has been placed with a foster carer who is willing and able to continue to care for them, the child should not be moved from the placement unless this is clearly in their best interests after taking into account their wishes and feelings, and following a review. Sometimes there are emergencies when remaining in the placement is impractical or puts other household members at risk.

A common reason for placements breaking down is that people find they are not well matched, rather than either the child or the foster carer being in any way to blame. When a placement comes to an end, foster carers, the child's social worker, the supervising social worker and other significant people need to work together to help the child to understand why they are moving, and to support them through the change.

There are particular factors to take into account in considering whether a child must be removed from a placement following an allegation, and these are considered in section 8 of this guide.

Things to think about: making and ending placements

Children's social workers and supervising social workers

	yes	no
Are matching procedures effective in meeting children's needs?	☐	☐
Does the fostering service only offer placements that are likely to meet a child's needs?	☐	☐
Where there are already other children placed, is the consent of their social workers always obtained before placing another child in the foster home?	☐	☐
Is a review always held before a change of placement takes place?	☐	☐

Foster carers

	yes	no
Do you always receive the information you need before a placement is made, or at the time of placement in an emergency?	☐	☐
If you do not get information you need, does your supervising social worker follow this up?	☐	☐

4) Planning for children in foster care

Care plans

Care Planning Placement and Case Review (England) Regulations 2010 regulations 4-8; Children Act 1989 Guidance and Regulations Volume 2: Care Planning, Placement and Case Review, chapter 2

The child's social worker is responsible for co-ordinating the plan for their care, but they do this in partnership with the child, their parents, and other members of the team around the child. This means that foster carers should contribute to care planning, including participating in meetings and reviews.

Every looked after child must have a care plan, which is regularly reviewed and updated. Care plans should ensure that everyone is clear about their responsibilities and what is being aimed for.

Care plans must include the:

- long-term plan, or 'permanence plan'
- health plan
- personal education plan (PEP)
- plan for contact
- placement plan (as described in section 5)
- name of the allocated Independent Reviewing Officer (IRO).

There are modified arrangements for children who receive only short break care. For young people who will be leaving care and need a pathway plan, this has to include the care plan.

A permanence plan must be agreed at the child's second review after they become looked after. Permanence can be achieved in a variety of ways, including a return home to parents, long-term fostering, a residence or child arrangements order, special guardianship or adoption.

Regulation 14

Guidance 3.27

Unless a court order or the placement plan says otherwise, fostering services have a duty to promote contact between a fostered child and their parents, relatives and friends, unless this is not practical or consistent with their welfare. Support should also be given where appropriate to promote contact with other people who are important to the child.

Standard 31

Foster carers are expected to help children to put forward their views and to understand the contents of their care plan, and should be supported to do so.

Reviews

Care plans have to be reviewed regularly to monitor how far outcomes have been achieved and to make changes to the plan in the light of current circumstances. The aim is always to make sure that the child's welfare is safeguarded and promoted. The minimum frequency of reviews is shown in the diagram below.

Maximum intervals between reviews

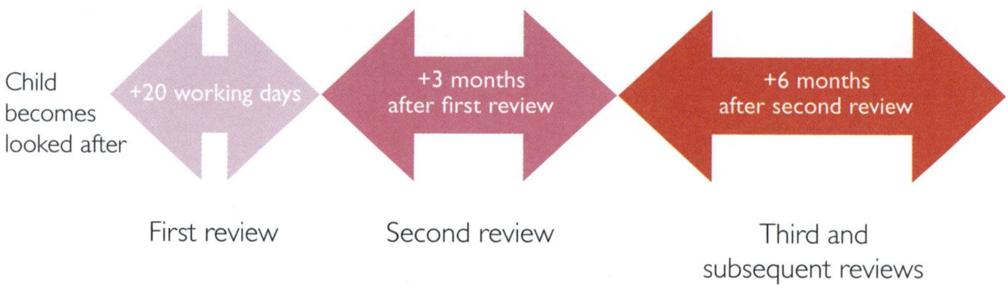

Standard 31; Care Planning Placement and Case Review (England) Regulations 2010 regulations 32-38; Children Act 1989 Guidance and Regulations Volume 2: Care Planning, Placement and Case Review, chapter 4; IRO Handbook

Reviews have to be chaired by an IRO, who is an experienced social worker independent of the people who are responsible for managing the child's case or allocating resources. Their task is to make sure that the care plan reflects the child's needs and also to monitor the implementation of the care plan. IROs have responsibilities to speak up for looked after children and, if necessary, to challenge other people if they feel that good practice is not being followed.

IRO Handbook 3.6

A review can be one meeting attended by all the relevant people, or a number of meetings with one central meeting attended by the IRO, child, social worker and some of the relevant adults. The IRO and the child's social worker, in consultation with the child, have to decide the best way to manage this before each review. As central members of the team around the child, foster carers have an important contribution to make to this planning.

Children Act 1989 Guidance and Regulations Volume 2; Care Planning, Placement and Case Review 4.25

IRO Handbook 3.21

Children Act 1989 Guidance and Regulations Volume 2: Care Planning, Placement and Case Review 4.23

The child, parents and foster carers should always be consulted about the timing and venue for the review to make sure that the right people are able to attend, and children should not have to miss school in order to be at their review. Reviews should take place at a venue where the child feels most comfortable and first consideration should be given to meeting at the foster home, although this may not always be appropriate (depending on who else will be attending). Foster carers should be invited to reviews, as otherwise they cannot provide effective day-to- day parenting and meet the expectations of the placement plan. If for any reason they are not present, the IRO must make sure that their views are taken into account at the review. Reviews should be held at a time and place that makes it possible for those who need to attend to do so.

People who should attend the child's review meeting

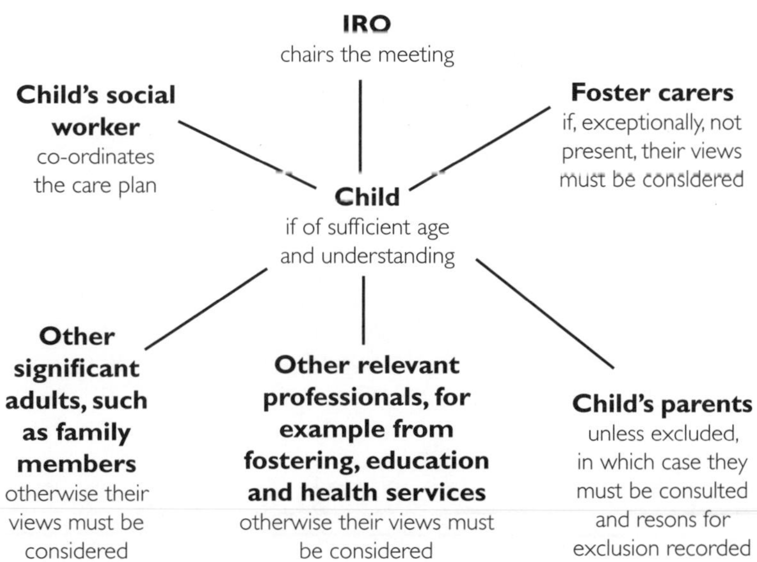

Social worker visits

Care Planning Placement and Case Review (England) Regulations 2010 regulations 28-31; Children Act 1989 Guidance and Regulations Volume 2: Care Planning, Placement and Case Review, 3.155 – 3.176

The child's social worker has to visit them as part of their supervision of the foster placement and to ensure that the child's welfare is still being safeguarded and promoted. As part of their visit, the child's social worker should give the foster carer any advice necessary about responding to the child's behaviour and identify any further support that is needed.

The **minimum** frequency at which the child's social worker must visit the child depends on the type of placement, as shown in the table below.

Minimum frequency of social worker visits to a fostered child

Type of foster placement	Minimum frequency of visits
All new placements	Within a week of placement
Foster carer has only temporary approval	Weekly until child's first review, then four-weekly
In placement for less than a year	Six-weekly
In placement for more than a year and this has been formally agreed as a permanent placement to last until age 18	Three-monthly (otherwise remains six-weekly)
All placements	Whenever reasonably requested by the child or foster carer

The social worker must see the child alone for at least some part of the visit, unless the child refuses or the social worker feels this would be inappropriate. The social worker has to write a report of their visit, but should also share information appropriately with the foster carer.

Things to think about: planning for children in foster care

Foster carers

	yes	no
Do you have up-to-date copies of children's care plans, including the permanence plan, health plan, personal education plan, plan for contact and placement plan?	☐	☐
Are all parts of the care plans reviewed within timescales and kept up to date?	☐	☐
Do you always contribute to children's reviews?	☐	☐
Are review meetings held at a time when you and others can attend?	☐	☐
Does every fostered child have a named IRO?	☐	☐
Are children visited by their social worker at least within minimum timescales?	☐	☐
Do social workers share information about visits appropriately with you?	☐	☐

Standard 31; Care Planning Placement and Case Review (England) Regulations 2010 regulation 9; Children Act 1989 Guidance and Regulations Volume 2: Care Planning, Placement and Case Review, 3.128-3.154

5) Placement plans and delegated authority

Placement plans

Every fostered child must have a care plan, which includes a placement plan. Placement plans are the key to making sure that everyone concerned is clear about the foster carer's role as part of the team around the individual child, and how the day-to-day parenting tasks will be shared between the carer and the local authority.

The child's social worker is responsible for making sure the placement plan is prepared, and the foster carer should be involved in this process as they have to agree to it and be given a copy. The best way to achieve an appropriate plan will be to hold a meeting that involves the foster carer, supervising social worker and the child's social worker and, depending on the circumstances, the child and their parents.

The placement plan has to be written before the child is placed with the foster carer, unless this is not 'reasonably practicable' in which case it must be drawn up within five working days of the start of the placement. For instance, it might not be practical to prepare the plan in advance when a child becomes looked after suddenly in an emergency, but it would not be acceptable to fail to prioritise drawing up a plan if the placement had been identified several days in advance. As the placement plan is an integral part of the care plan it is, as a minimum, reviewed every time the care plan is reviewed. It should therefore be seen very much as a 'living document'.

Care Planning Placement and Case Review (England) Regulations 2010 Schedule 2

The regulations spell out in detail everything that the placement plan must cover. Key elements are:

- how the child's day-to-day needs will be met
- arrangements for health and education
- arrangements for the social worker to visit
- contact arrangements, including any decisions to refuse contact
- arrangements for delegating authority to the foster carer
- the name of the child's IRO.

Delegated authority

Standard 7. Delegation of authority: Amendments to the Children Act 1989 Guidance and Regulations, July 2013

From the start of the placement, foster carers need to know what authority they have to make decisions, even if this needs to be reviewed soon afterwards. The child's social worker is responsible for ensuring that arrangements for delegated authority are made clear, in consultation with the foster carer and supervising social worker, through preparing the placement plan.

It is expected that authority for day-to-day decision making about a fostered child will be delegated to foster carers unless there is a valid reason not to do so. This includes routine decisions about health, education and leisure activities. Who should have authority to take particular decisions will depend in part on the child's permanence plan. There may be some significant decisions, such as surgery, which are not appropriate to delegate to the foster carer, but their views should still be taken into account.

It is vital that everyone is aware of what delegated authority foster carers have been given in respect of any child, and as a minimum the placement plan must always make clear who has the authority to take decisions in six key areas of the child's day-to-day life:

Care Planning Placement and Case Review and Fostering Services(Miscellaneous Amendments) Regulations 2013, regulation 4

- medical and dental treatment
- education
- leisure and home life
- faith and religious observance
- use of social media
- any other areas of decision making considered relevant with respect to the particular child.

As far as possible, foster carers should be able to make the same sort of everyday decisions which other parents make, such as agreeing to sleepovers with friends, going on school trips or having a holiday with their friends or a relative of the foster carer. There is no requirement for DBS checks to be made before a child has a sleepover or goes

The Fostering Network publishes a suite of resources on delegated authority, which are free for members to download from **www.fostering.net**

away on holiday, unless there are particular circumstances which make this necessary.

The Education Act 1996 definition of a parent covers the role of a foster carer, so foster carers should be treated like parents with respect to information provided by a school, including being invited to meetings about the child and consenting to participation in school activities.

Depending on their age and understanding, young people may be deemed competent to consent to their own medical treatment.

Local authorities have to publish a policy which sets out their approach to the delegation of authority to foster carers and residential workers caring for children. The policy has to take account of the need to maximise wherever possible the delegation of authority to foster carers. It should be made widely available.

Things to think about:
placement plans and delegated authority

Children's social workers and supervising social workers

	yes	no
Is there a placement plan in respect of every child placed with foster carers?		
Are foster carers always involved in drawing up the placement plan?		
Do placement plans always cover the six key areas of delegated authority?		
Are placement plans kept up to date and relevant?		

Foster carers

	yes	no
Are you clear about arrangements for delegated authority in respect of all the children you care for?		
Are you able to make day to day decisions affecting your foster children, or else clear why not?		
Are children ever singled out because they have to get permission from their social worker to go on school trips or have sleepovers at their friends?		
Have you read the local authority's policy on delegated authority?		

6) Listening to children

Child's wishes, feelings and personal identity

Standards 1 and 2; Guidance 3.31 – 3.37

The standards and guidance require that children's views, wishes and feelings should be listened to and acted on, unless this is against their interests or adversely affects other members of the fostering household. If their views cannot be acted on, it is important that social workers and foster carers help them to understand the reasons for this.

Children should be helped to develop a positive view of themselves and to understand their identity and background. Foster carers need to respect diversity and are expected to encourage children to exercise choice in the food that they eat and the clothes that they wear, within the context of normal family life. Children should be given a personal allowance which is appropriate to their age and understanding, taking into account what is said in the placement plan.

Foster carers have to agree to care for a child as if they were a child of their own family, and so are normally expected to treat the child in the same way as their own children. This often poses particular problems, which may need to be addressed in the placement plan. Social workers and others have to bear in mind that all families are different, and what is appropriate or possible in one family may not be in another, so a standard approach may be unhelpful.

Representations, complaints and advocacy

Regulation 18; Standard 1; Guidance 3.38-3.42

Children in foster care must be told about the representations and complaints procedure, and their right to advocacy. This information will be included in the children's guide to the fostering service, but social workers and foster carers should also make sure that children are aware of it. Children must be allowed privacy to contact an advocate and should be able to make private telephone calls, or safely access a range of relevant websites, in order to seek advice and help.

Guidance 3.85

Things to think about: listening to children

Children's social workers and supervising social workers

	yes	no
Do you help foster carers to meet the diverse range of children's needs within the context of family life?	☐	☐
Do children's views, wishes and feelings influence their care plans?	☐	☐

Foster carers

	yes	no
Do the children you care for understand how to make a complaint or how to get in touch with an advocate?	☐	☐
Are children able to make private phone calls?	☐	☐
Do you help children to exercise choice in the food they eat and the clothes they wear?	☐	☐

7) Health, leisure and education

Good health

Regulation 15; Standard 6; Guidance 3.49-3.62

Fostering services have a duty to promote the physical and mental health and wellbeing of children. In conjunction with the children's social workers, they must make sure that children in foster care are registered with a GP and see a dentist regularly, as well as having support including special equipment required for any particular health needs. It is important for foster carers to be aware of the contents of the child's health plan, which is part of the care plan, so that they can provide appropriate care. This information should be supplied by the child's social worker.

The Fostering Network publishes a Medical Treatment: authorisation to give consent *card, which allows fostering services and parents to pass on the right to sign for medical treatment to foster carers*

A fostering service must also have a policy on the administration of medication, and foster carers should have training in this as well as in general health and hygiene issues and first aid. Wherever possible, children should be helped to manage their own prescribed medication, but medication should only be accessible to those for whom it is prescribed. When a child is placed, their social worker must make sure that the foster carer is given appropriate authorisation to administer first aid and non-prescription medication and to consent to other medical or preventive treatment as written in the placement plan.

Foster carers should encourage children to lead healthy lifestyles and to take part in positive activities which contribute to physical and mental health.

Leisure activity

Standard 7; Guidance 3.115-3.117

It is important for looked after children to have access to a wide range of leisure activities, which helps them to enjoy their interests and develop self-confidence. Foster carers should encourage children to participate in normal activities in the same way that any reasonable parent would. They must be aware of the authority that they have to make decisions about activities, leisure interests and social events, and these must be included in arrangements for delegated authority in the placement plan.

Delegation of authority: Amendments to the Children Act 1989 Guidance and Regulations, July 2013

Where risk assessments have been routinely carried out by those organising an activity, such as school trips or activity breaks, decision making should be delegated to foster carers. There is no expectation that local authorities should duplicate risk assessments.

Educational achievement

Regulation 16; Standard 8; Guidance 3.100-3.114

Fostering services have a duty to promote the educational achievement of children and so foster carers must be given support to do so. There must be an education policy, and foster carers should help children to achieve good school attendance and be clear about their role in implementing the child's personal education plan. They must be fully involved in educational planning for the children they foster. Foster carers should keep in regular contact with the child's school or college, attend parents' meetings, advocate for the child as necessary, and make sure that the child has space to complete their homework.

Fostering services should ensure that children placed have any equipment necessary to support their education, including access to a computer.

Care Planning Placement and Case Review (England) Regulations 2010 regulation 10; Children Act 1989 Guidance and Regulations Volume 2: Care Planning, Placement and Case Review, 2.77

Wherever possible, foster placements should be made which will not disrupt a child's education, particularly by requiring a change of school. If a placement is proposed that would disrupt a child's education at key stage 4, this has to be authorised by a nominated senior officer of the local authority.

Things to think about: health, education and leisure

Children's social workers

Are placements that will disrupt a child's education at key stage 4 appropriately authorised?

Foster carers

Do you have copies of children's health plans?

Do you have any difficulty implementing the policy on administration of medication?

Are you clear about arrangements for giving consent to medical treatment?

Are you involved in preparing children's personal education plans?

Do you attend meetings about children's education?

8) Safeguarding children

Suitability to work with children

Regulations 20 and 21; Standard 13; Guidance 4.5-4.15

The regulations and NMS contain requirements that are designed to ensure that staff, foster carers, panel members and others concerned with the fostering service are suitable to work with children. These arrangements include identity and DBS checks, and references. There must also be a whistleblowing policy. A fostering service has to demonstrate that it follows good recruitment practice in all aspects of its work.

Promoting positive behaviour and taking risks

Regulation 13; Standard 3; Guidance 3.96-3.99

Foster carers are expected to promote positive behaviour in children through the care they provide, and to help to manage challenging behaviour through building positive relationships rather than relying on punishment. Every fostering service must have a policy about acceptable measures of control, restraint and discipline, which foster carers have to follow. This must be made clear to the child's social worker before a placement is made. Corporal punishment is not allowed. Restraint can only be used in exceptional circumstances when it is necessary to prevent a child being injured or serious damage to property.

Foster carers have to be given all the relevant information about the child to help them with this, including information about previous challenging behaviour and advice about how this might be handled in the future. If this is not provided by the child's social worker, the fostering service must follow this up.

The fostering service must provide training in the positive care and control of children, with an emphasis on de-escalating difficulties.

Standard 4.4

As well as promoting the safety and welfare of children in their care, foster carers have to support and encourage children to take appropriate risks as part of normal growing up and to learn from their mistakes. They must help children to keep themselves safe, including when using the internet or social media. This means that children's social workers have to support fostering services to adopt a measured approach to risk assessment, while making sure children are protected from harm.

Going missing

Regulation 13; Standard 5; Guidance 3.88-3.94

Supervising social workers need to make sure that foster carers understand the policy of their service about children who go missing or are absent from the home without permission. Foster carers must not use restraint to stop a child leaving the home unless this is unavoidable to prevent the child being injured or serious damage to property. When children do go missing, the child's social worker and supervising social worker need to support the foster carer to follow agreed protocols, and to consider what action is required to prevent this happening again.

Allegations against foster carers

Standard 22; Guidance 3.68-3.81

Any allegation made by a child must be taken seriously and investigated, although sometimes false allegations are made. Fostering services must have a safeguarding policy, which includes an explanation of how allegations will be investigated, including the independent support that foster carers will be offered and what allowances and fees will be paid if they are unable to take placements during the investigation.

Guidance 3.73

Foster carers must be given appropriate information about any allegation made against them and the reasons for an unplanned move of a child. The possible risk of harm to children posed by an accused person needs to be effectively evaluated and managed; foster carers must not be 'suspended' automatically or without careful thought.

Standard 22.7

Every fostering service has a senior manager who is responsible for managing allegations, liaising with the appropriate person in the local authority and making sure that the person against whom an allegation has been made is kept informed of the progress of the investigation. At the end of the investigation a comprehensive summary of the allegation, investigation and outcome has to be produced and a copy provided to the subject of the allegation. The foster carer's suitability to continue to foster will then be reviewed, taking account of the fostering service's

Standard 22.8

written policy on the circumstances in which a foster carer's approval should be terminated in the interests of children.

Standard 22.10

A distinction has to be made between an investigation into an allegation of harm and discussion about standards of care. If an investigation finds no evidence of harm, it must not be turned into a consideration of poor standards of care: these should be treated separately.

Guidance 3.78-3.79

A summary of any allegation and its resolution will be kept on a foster carer's records, but unsubstantiated, unfounded and malicious allegations should not be included in references.

Things to think about: safeguarding children

Fostering services

How are foster carers helped to de-escalate challenging behaviour?
Do all foster carers and staff understand the whistleblowing policy?
Is independent support offered to foster carers during an investigation?
Are foster carers given a summary report upon completion of an investigation into an allegation?
Are investigations of possible harm kept separate from concerns about poor standards?

Foster carers	yes	no
Do you understand the policy on acceptable measures of control, restraint and discipline?		
Can you support children to take acceptable risks?		
Do you know how to follow the 'missing from care' procedures?		
Are you aware of the policy concerning investigations into allegations?		
Do you know in what circumstances you might be considered no longer suitable to foster?		

Standard 12; Guidance 3.118 -3.125; Children Act 1989 Guidance and Regulations Volume 3: Planning Transition to Adulthood for Care Leavers

9) Moving into adulthood

As young people approach adulthood foster carers should increasingly support them to develop the skills they will need as they become more independent, working with the young person's social worker or personal adviser to implement their pathway plan. Fostering services should make sure that foster carers have appropriate training and support in this task.

The expectation is that young people get practical, financial and emotional support through their transition to adulthood, as their peers would receive from their own parents. They have to be given a personal adviser to co-ordinate this support, and it may be agreed that the young person's foster carer or former foster carer is able to fulfil a part of that role. Whatever their role, the foster carer should liaise with the child's social worker, IRO and personal adviser about their readiness for moving into greater independence.

The plan for helping the young person to make the transition is called their 'pathway plan' and, so long as they remain looked after by the local authority, this process will include the care plan.

Staying put

Young people under 18 should not have to leave foster care unless they feel ready to do so. Even at age 18 many young people are not ready to leave, and 'staying put' arrangements mean that young people are supported to remain living with their foster carers beyond their 18th birthday if both parties agree to this. Such arrangements should be promoted by the young person's local authority, but do not need their authorisation to go ahead. Whenever staying put arrangements are possible, the details should be included in the pathway plan.

Staying put is not fostering, because the young people are adults and no longer looked after by the local authority. However the local authority has a legal duty to support both the young person and the staying put carer unless, very exceptionally, the arrangement is not consistent with the young person's welfare. This has to include financial support to cover all reasonable costs of supporting the young person to remain

Children and Families Act 2014 s98

living with them. Staying put arrangements last until the young person is 21, or until they stop living with their former foster carer if that is earlier.

Staying put carers might also continue to foster other children, in which case the young person on staying put is regarded as an adult member of the fostering household. In these circumstances the regulations require them to have a DBS check.

A good practice guide to staying put can be downloaded from ***www.ncb.org.uk/stayingput***

Local authorities and fostering services should have staying put policies, setting out how they make arrangements for young people and carers.

Things to think about: moving into adulthood

Do foster carers receive appropriate preparation and training to support young people through the transition to adulthood?

Do recruitment and assessment procedures prepare foster carers for the possibility of continuing to provide care beyond 18?

Are there clear arrangements for supporting foster carers who continue to provide care to young people who they previously fostered?

10) Short breaks

Some foster carers provide a series of short breaks to help children to remain within their own families. These services are mainly provided for disabled children, but are also used by other children in need. Fostering services and foster carers must be sure that they have clear information about the circumstances of any child receiving short breaks, because even if the child stays longer than 24 hours with the foster carer they may not always be a looked after child. Short breaks can be provided either under section 17(6) or section 20(4) of the Children Act 1989. The number of days of care that is provided does not, in itself, affect whether or not the child is looked after, although if they are then it may change the way in which the case is reviewed.

If a child is not looked after the short break is not a foster placement, and therefore foster carers will need clarification about how any payments they receive are treated for tax or welfare benefits purposes.

Regulation 42; Standards 2.5, 2.7, 9 & 12

When children receive only short breaks their parents retain the main responsibility for planning for them, and so some of the regulations and standards do not apply.

Things to think about: short breaks

Is it always made clear to everyone whether or not the child is an accommodated child placed under fostering regulations?
Are foster carers given clear information about their status and responsibilities regarding tax or welfare benefits if they receive payments for a child who is not looked after?

11) Parent and child arrangements

Sometimes arrangements are made for a parent and their child to both live with a foster carer: often this is to enable a parenting assessment to be made of a mother and baby. Everyone concerned needs to be clear about the nature of the arrangements made in a particular case, as they are not always covered by the fostering regulations and NMS. If the parent is under 18, and both the parent and child are looked after children, both will be foster placements. However, sometimes only the child or the parent is a looked after child, and so is placed as a foster child. If neither the parent nor the child is a looked after child the arrangements will not be covered by the fostering regulations. In any situation where the parent is aged 18 or over they are not 'fostered', so foster carers will need clarification about any tax or welfare benefit implications.

Whatever the situation, it is always important to clarify the respective roles of the foster carer and the parent in relation to the child, and the fostering service needs to consider the additional responsibilities of the foster carer and any further training, support or insurance cover that the foster carer might need.

Annex B of the statutory guidance explains more fully the requirements in different situations.

Things to think about: parent and child arrangements

Is the parent a looked after child, placed under the fostering regulations?

Is the child a looked after child, placed under the fostering regulations?

Are the responsibilities of the foster carer and the parent – in respect of the child – clear?

Are foster carers given clear information about their status with regard to tax and welfare benefits if they receive payments for an adult, or for a child not looked after?

Regulations 3 & 4; Standard 16; Guidance 4.1-4.5

12) Statement of purpose and children's guide

Statement of purpose

Family and Friends Care: Statutory Guidance for Local Authorities, 4.44

Fostering services have to publish a 'statement of purpose', which spells out their aims and objectives and lists the services and facilities that are provided. This includes any provision for family and friends foster carers and for parent and child arrangements.

The statement of purpose should guide all of the work of the fostering service, its staff and foster carers. It should explain for everyone how the service goes about meeting the needs of children and so help people to understand how they can best work as a team and make use of the support available to children and foster carers. Although there is no statutory requirement to supply a copy direct to the social worker of children placed, it is important to do so in order that they can be satisfied that the placement is likely to meet the child's needs and be aware of the roles of other people who will be in the team working with the child.

Children's guide

There is also a requirement to publish a children's guide to the fostering service, which includes a summary of the statement of purpose and of the representation and complaints procedure. It must be produced in a format which is appropriate to the age, understanding and communication needs of children, so in practice this means that it is usually necessary to produce several versions of the guide aimed at different age groups, and including formats accessible to those with learning or communication difficulties.

Review of statement of purpose and children's guide

The regulations merely require the statement of purpose and the children's guide to be kept under review, and revised when appropriate. However, the guidance says that both must be reviewed at least annually, although there is no particular method by which the review must take place. The table opposite explains who must be sent copies, including when either document is revised.

Requirements for the statement of purpose and children's guide

Requirements	**Statement of purpose**	**Children's guide**
Publication	Must be published on website, if there is one	Good practice to publish on website
Send to all foster carers?	Not required, but good practice	Must be sent
Send to children placed?	Not required	Must be sent at the time of placement, subject to age and understanding
Copy to Ofsted	Must be sent	Must be sent
Available on request to:	• anyone working for the fostering service • prospective and approved foster carers • children placed • parents of children placed • anyone else (good practice)	Anyone interested (good practice)
Provide to children's social workers and others working with children in foster care	Good practice	Good practice

Things to think about: statement of purpose and children's guide

Children's social workers

	yes	no
Do you understand the aims and objectives of the fostering service?	☐	☐

Fostering services

	yes	no
Is there an up-to-date statement of purpose?	☐	☐
Is the statement of purpose child focused and does it show how the fostering service will meet outcomes for children?	☐	☐
Is there an up-to-date children's guide?	☐	☐
Is the children's guide available in different formats for children of different ages and abilities?	☐	☐
Does the children's guide explain how to make a complaint or contact an advocate or Ofsted?	☐	☐
Does the fostering service always operate in accordance with its statement of purpose?	☐	☐

Foster carers

	yes	no
Do you have access to a copy of the statement of purpose and are you familiar with what it contains?	☐	☐
Do you help children placed with you to understand the children's guide to the fostering service?	☐	☐

Standard 14; Guidance 5.1-5.25

13) Fostering panels

Purpose

Regulation 25

Every fostering service must set up at least one fostering panel to carry out the functions listed in the table below. A fostering panel can be established jointly by any two or more fostering service providers (local authorities or IFPs). A local authority can have a permanence panel, which could cover both adoption and fostering matters, so long as the requirements of both the adoption and fostering regulations are complied with.

Fostering panels play a very important quality assurance role, providing objectivity and having the ability to challenge practice that is felt to fall short of the regulations or NMS, or not to be in the interests of children. They bring a degree of independence from the fostering service and cannot make decisions themselves, but rather make recommendations that the fostering service decision maker must take into account. They are also required to give regular feedback to the fostering service.

Functions of a fostering panel

1	To consider applications for approval and recommend whether or not a person is suitable to act as a foster carer, and if so the terms on which they should be approved – eg number and age of children to be placed.
2	To consider the first review of newly-approved foster carers, and any subsequent reviews referred to it by the fostering service, and recommend whether or not they remain suitable to act as foster carers, and if the terms of the approval remain appropriate.
3	To oversee the conduct of assessments carried out by the fostering service.
4	To monitor and advise on the procedures for undertaking reviews of foster carers.
5	To consider any case where written representations have been received regarding qualifying determinations about approvals, reviews or terminations of approval.
6	To give advice and make recommendations on any other matters or cases referred to the panel by the fostering service.

Membership

Regulation 23

Every fostering service must keep a list of people who have the appropriate qualifications and experience to serve as panel members. In the regulations this is called the 'central list' and in practical terms it is a mechanism for keeping track of the pool of people from whom panel membership can be drawn. When setting up a panel to deal with one or more items of business, the members who will form that panel have to be drawn from the service's central list of people. If a panel is not able to make a recommendation on a particular case (perhaps because they need more information or advice) and the meeting has to be adjourned, the same panel should reconvene at the second and any subsequent meetings until the case has been finalised.

Membership of a particular panel should consist of people with qualities relevant to the issues to be considered. People who are likely to make a positive contribution include those with knowledge and experience of:

- being a foster carer, including family and friends foster care and short breaks
- living in foster care
- assessing and supporting foster carers
- care planning for looked after children
- education of looked after children
- being a son or daughter of a foster carer
- health and wellbeing of looked after children
- corporate parenting – eg as local authority elected members
- having a child in foster care.

The intention of the central list is to allow fostering services flexibility in constituting their fostering panels. Having a pool of people with different skills, experience and qualifications to draw from allows for the most appropriate members to consider the cases assigned to the panel. It also reduces the likelihood of a panel meeting having to be postponed because, for example, a panel can more easily be set up specifically to consider any urgent business. Knowledgeable and experienced members can be retained without the need to wait for a vacancy to occur to appoint a new member to the list. Retaining a core membership across panels will, however, help them to function cohesively and with a level of consistency. There is no limit on the maximum size of fostering panels, although fostering services should avoid panels that are too large as they may become unwieldy to chair and intimidating to foster carers and social workers attending.

A member of a fostering panel cannot also be involved in making decisions about the approval of a foster carer. So if, for instance, a supervising social worker has undertaken an assessment of a foster carer or their team manager has been consulted about the application or has signed off the assessment report, neither person should be a member of the panel that considers that assessment report. Either person could, however, be on the central list and sit on a panel considering cases in which they have had no decision making role.

Standard 14.1

Panel members can be appointed for whatever period the fostering service feels appropriate, but the central list should be kept under regular review. Each fostering service should have a clear policy and procedure regarding recruitment to, and maintenance of, the central list. It is appropriate for the decision maker to take responsibility for this.

Chair and vice chairs

Regulation 23

Whenever a panel is set up from people on the central list, one of those members must be appointed as the chair and either one or two must be appointed as vice chairs. A vice chair could chair any meetings of the particular panel if the appointed chair is unable to attend – for example, if a case is adjourned to another date.

In order to ensure that the panel is not unduly influenced by the fostering service in carrying out its quality assurance role, only an independent person can be appointed to chair a panel. A person is not independent if they are a foster carer for the same fostering service, or they are an employee or trustee of the IFP, or they are an elected member (councillor) of the local authority, or they are employed by it in the fostering service or in a role relating to the protection or placement of children.

A vice chair does not have to be independent, but the quality assurance role will be better supported if they are.

The role of panel chair is central to the effective operation of the fostering panel as they are responsible for ensuring that all members of the panel are able to contribute to discussion and that appropriate recommendations are made that focus on the needs of children. The chair is also responsible for ensuring that full and accurate minutes are kept, which explain clearly what was discussed and why particular recommendations were made, to inform the decision maker in their own consideration.

Quorum

Regulation 24

A fostering panel can only deal with any business if at least five members are present (or six in the case of a joint panel), including either the chair or a vice chair, and a social worker who has at least three years' relevant post-qualifying experience. Relevant experience means child care social work that includes direct experience of fostering either within a fostering service or in placing and supervising children in foster care. A social worker panel member might be expected to demonstrate an understanding of current legislation, policy and good practice in relation to fostering matters, and to advise the panel accordingly. They do not have to be employed by the fostering service, although they can be.

Guidance 5.7

If the panel chair is not present at a particular meeting and the vice chair is not independent, then at least one other member must be independent.

Performance of panel members

Everyone appointed to the central list of panel members has to be informed in writing of their performance objectives, including participation in induction and training, and safeguarding the confidentiality of records and information. Panel members' performance against these objectives is reviewed annually. The service's decision maker reviews the performance of the panel chair and so can attend some panel meetings as an observer. Views about the chair's performance should be sought from other panel members and from those who attend panel meetings, such as prospective foster carers and social workers who present reports to the panel. For all other panel members, the panel chair conducts the performance review.

Guidance 5.14-5.18

Panel members can resign from the panel at any time by giving one month's notice in writing, although members should be encouraged to give as much notice as possible. Where a fostering service regards a member of a fostering panel as unsuitable or unable to continue on the panel, they may terminate their appointment by giving notice in writing. A person can resign from a fostering panel, or have their membership terminated, but remain on the central list. A person can ask to be removed from the list by giving one month's notice, or the fostering service can remove the person from the list also by giving one month's notice.

Members of fostering panels can be paid a reasonable fee, as well as expenses incurred in connection with attending panel meetings and related activity. These can be either an annual amount or a fee per meeting, and can take account of preparation time for panel meetings.

Information needs

Panel members must be given all the information they need at least five working days in advance of panel meetings although, depending on the substance of this, longer may be required. Panels may request any further information, including legal or medical advice, which they feel may help them to make a recommendation. The fostering service must

Standard 14

obtain any information that the panel feels necessary, and provide any other assistance the panel requests, so far as is reasonably practicable.

There is no requirement to appoint a legal adviser or medical adviser to a fostering panel, but to do so is likely to assist the panel when it feels such advice to be necessary.

Attending panel

Standard 14.5

Foster carers and prospective foster carers have the right to attend the fostering panel whenever their approval is being discussed, and for their views to be heard and considered. They can take a supporter with them. Subject to the need to safeguard children and having to deal sensitively with third party information, they should be able to read in advance any reports concerning them that are being presented to panel and to make any further written submission themselves.

Things to think about: fostering panels

Is there a clear policy about maintenance of the central list?

How do panels give quality assurance feedback?

Do panel members receive papers at least five working days before meetings?

How are applicants and foster carers helped to attend panel? Can they bring a supporter, and are they listened to?

What medical and legal advice do panels get?

Are accurate minutes kept that record panel members' views and the reasons for recommendations?

Are panels equipped to make competent recommendations?

Standard 13

14) Approving and reviewing foster carers

Assessment

Assessment and Approval of Foster Carers: Amendments to the Children Act 1989 Guidance and Regulations (July 2013) Care Planning Placement and Case Review and Fostering Services (Miscellaneous Amendments) Regulations 2013 Standard 13

The Fostering Network publishes *The Skills to Foster: assessment materials* – for more information visit **www.fostering resources.co.uk**

Applying to foster

Foster carers care for the majority of children in England who are looked after by local authorities, yet there remains a significant shortfall in the number of approved foster carers. People who express an interest in becoming foster carers should be treated fairly, without prejudice, openly and with respect, and given appropriate information, including about the assessment process and the timescale. Through the assessment they should be helped to understand the challenges they are likely to face, and the competencies and strengths they have or need to develop. They should be considered in terms of their capacity to look after children in a safe and responsible way that meets the child's developmental needs.

Some people will be automatically barred from becoming a foster carer because either they or an adult member of their household have been cautioned for, or convicted of, certain offences committed at or above the age of 18. It is important to check any offences carefully against the details given in Regulation 26 and Schedule 4.

Standard 10.6

Foster homes must provide adequate space to care for a fostered child. Children aged over three should have their own bedroom, but if this is not possible sharing must be agreed by the children's social workers after taking account of the children's wishes, the potential for bullying, and any history of abuse or abusive behaviour. The decision making process about sharing a bedroom has to be recorded.

No one has a right to be a foster carer, and decisions must always focus on the interests of the child. The regulations were amended in 2013 to require a two stage approach to fostering assessments. If someone interested in becoming a foster carer does not fulfil the recruitment criteria of the service they approach, the service may decline to undertake an assessment of their suitability. This might be, for instance, because of where they live, or the age of child they would be able to

FOSTERING SERVICES (ENGLAND) REGULATIONS 2011 SCHEDULE 3 (REVISED FROM 1 JULY 2013)

Information as to prospective foster parent ('X') and other members of their household and family.

PART 1

1. Full name, address and date of birth.
2. Details of health (supported by a medical report).
3. Particulars of any other adult members of the household.
4. Particulars of the children in the family, whether or not members of the household, and any other children in the household.
5. Particulars of their accommodation.
6. The outcome of any request or application made by them or any other member of their household to foster or adopt children, or for registration as an early years provider or later years provider under Part 3 of the Childcare Act 2006(b), including particulars of any previous approval or refusal of approval relating to them or to any other member of the household.
7. If X has, in the preceding twelve months, been a foster parent approved by another fostering service provider, the name and address of that fostering service provider.
8. Names and addresses of two persons who will provide personal references for X.
9. In relation to X and any other member of X's household who is aged 18 or over, an enhanced criminal record certificate issued under section 113B of the Police Act 1997 which includes suitability information relating to children (within the meaning of section 113BA(2) of that Act).
10. Details of current, and any previous, marriage, civil partnership or similar relationship.

PART 2

11. Details of personality.
12. Religious persuasion, and capacity to care for a child from any particular religious persuasion.
13. Racial origin, cultural and linguistic background and capacity to care for a child from any particular racial origin or cultural or linguistic background.
14. Past and present employment or occupation, standard of living, leisure activities and interests.
15. Previous experience (if any) of caring for their own and other children.
16. Skills, competence and potential relevant to their capacity to care effectively for a child placed with them.

foster, or some other factor. Otherwise the service should proceed to stage one of the assessment process.

Regulation 26 as amended

Assessment stage one

Stage one requires the fostering service – 'as soon as reasonably practicable' – to collect information about the applicant and their household, and to undertake routine checks. These are listed in Part 1 of the revised Schedule 3 of the fostering regulations and include a medical report and enhanced DBS certificates. The local authority where the applicant lives must also be consulted during stage one.

If the applicant has been an approved foster carer for another fostering service within the last twelve months, there is a requirement to request a written reference from that fostering service. Whilst there is no legal requirement for the service to supply such a reference, it is clearly best practice to do so. In any case, the records of the fostering service will be open to viewing by the service which is undertaking the assessment.

Written reports of interviews with two personal referees must be obtained during stage one. This does not apply when a written reference has been obtained from another fostering service as described above, but even then the assessing service may choose to interview the personal referees if they feel that it would be helpful to do so. Services may sometimes feel that it is appropriate to further interview personal referees during stage two of the assessment when more is known about the applicant's personal qualities and experience.

Assessment stage two

Stage two of the assessment focuses on the applicant's skills and experience, and requires consideration of the matters listed in Part 2 of the revised Schedule 3. When the assessment is completed the applicant must be given a copy and has ten working days to make any written observations, after which the report, any observations of the applicant and any other relevant information has to be presented to the fostering panel. There is no specific requirement about the format of the report to the fostering panel, but the Fostering Network's The Skills to Foster Assessment Report Form provides a framework for this.

The assessment report should be presented to a fostering panel within eight months of the application.

Standard 14.4

Stages one and two can be run in parallel: there is no requirement to complete stage one before starting stage two. This may be useful in reducing delay if collection of some of the stage one information is likely to take some time. It is, however, important to be clear which information relates to which stage, since there are different arrangements for terminating an assessment if stage one has not been completed.

The Fostering Network's *The Skills to Foster* provides a comprehensive training package which forms part of the assessment process

Training is usually included as part of the assessment process, to help applicants to understand the role of a foster carer and to equip themselves for the task. This may be provided at either stage of the assessment.

Terminating a fostering assessment

An applicant can withdraw his or her application to become a foster carer at any time during the assessment, but otherwise an assessment can only be terminated in accordance with the regulations.

If information comes to light as part of stage one which shows that an applicant is unsuitable to be a foster carer, the assessment can be terminated if the service's decision maker notifies the applicant in writing. The latest point at which this can be done is ten working days after all the stage one information has been obtained. If the applicant is not given written notification within this timescale, then the assessment can only be terminated in accordance with the requirements of stage two.

During stage two, if information comes to light that an applicant is unlikely to be suitable to become a foster carer, a report can be prepared describing progress with the assessment and the reasons that the applicant is thought unlikely to be suitable. This is referred to as a 'brief report', by which is meant that it does not reflect a completed assessment. There is no prescribed length or format. As with a full assessment, the applicant must be given a copy of the brief report and given ten working days to give their observations, which will then be presented to the fostering panel with the report itself. Taking account of the panel's recommendation, the decision maker must then determine whether the full assessment should be completed or to issue a qualifying determination stating the intention not to give approval as a foster carer, as explained later in this section.

Support networks

Sometimes other people, such as babysitters or members of the foster carer's extended family, play an important role in supporting foster carers. It is good practice to include in assessment reports information about the support which applicants will be given by family and friends. There is no requirement for such people to be approved as foster carers, even if they sometimes provide care for a fostered child who remains formally placed with their usual foster carer – for instance a foster carer's own parent who looks after their fostered child while they have a weekend away. Professional judgment has to be used to decide whether criminal record or any other checks might be required in specific circumstances, or whether the foster carers can be given delegated authority to make decisions about suitability. If however the child is being formally placed by the local authority with the relative instead of with their usual foster carer, then that person must be approved as a foster carer.

The decision maker

Standard 14

Every fostering service must appoint a 'decision maker' to make decisions for the fostering service about the approval of foster carers. A decision maker cannot delegate their authority to anyone else but more than one person can be appointed, which may be helpful for instance to ensure that holiday periods are covered. The decision maker must take into account all of the information available, always including any recommendation of the fostering panel or the Independent Review Mechanism (IRM). Decision makers should be clear about the reasons for their decisions, particularly if these differ from panel recommendations.

Standard 23.12

The decision maker should be a senior member of staff – or in the case of an IFP could be a trustee or a director of the agency – who is a social worker who has at least three years post-qualifying experience in child care social work and has knowledge of child care law and practice. If necessary the decision maker could be employed specifically for the role, so long as they carry the necessary authority on behalf of the fostering service. They cannot also be a member of the fostering panel but there are no other restrictions.

Standard 14.9

Regulation 27(4); Guidance 5,23

Standard 14.10

The decision maker should make decisions within seven working days of receiving the panel's recommendation by way of the final minutes. It is important that the decision maker considers the panel minutes before reaching a decision as they will need to demonstrate the information taken into account and the reasons for their decision. The decision maker is not able to discuss the panel's deliberations and recommendations with the chair or any other member of panel since they are barred from involvement in any decision about the approval of a foster carer. Once the decision has been made by the decision maker, this must be given verbally to the applicant or foster carer within two working days and confirmed in writing within five working days.

Refusing approval

Regulation 27

If, having taken account of the panel's recommendations, the decision maker considers that an applicant is unsuitable to become a foster carer they must send them a 'qualifying determination'. This is a written notice of their proposed decision giving their reasons, and explaining that they have 28 days within which to make representation to the decision maker or to apply to the Independent Review Mechanism (IRM) for an independent review on behalf of the Secretary of State. If no response is received within 28 days the decision maker is free to implement the decision.

If within the 28 day period the applicant makes representation to the fostering service, this must be considered by the fostering panel and the decision maker must then take account of the panel recommendation in reaching a decision. If an application is made to the IRM then within

Qualifying determinations and the Independent Review Mechanism

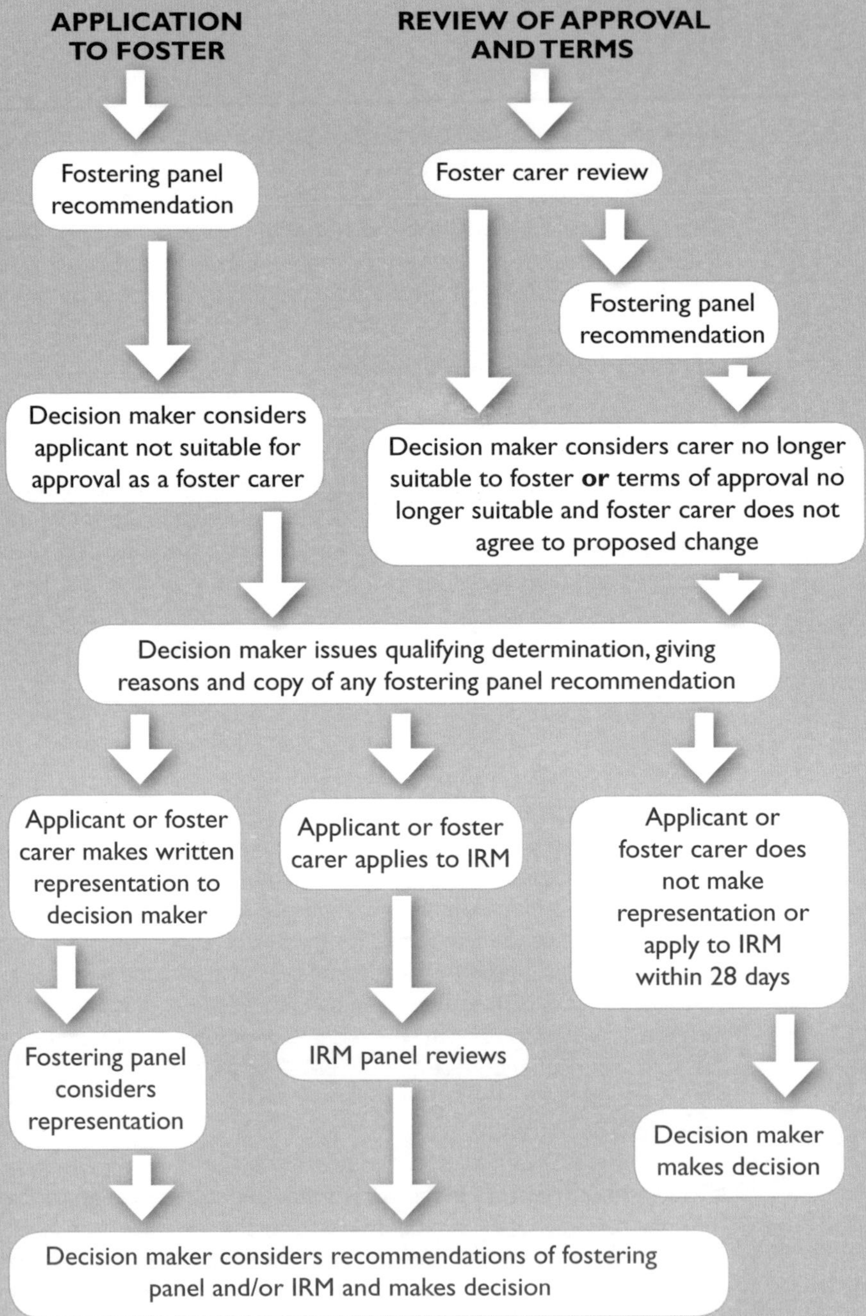

10 working days the fostering service must supply the documentation that was considered by the fostering panel, as well as any relevant information received since and copies of the qualifying determination. The decision maker must take account of the recommendations of both the IRM and the fostering panel in reaching a decision. This process is shown in the flow chart opposite.

Terms of approval

Regulation 27

Foster carers must be informed in writing of any terms of their approval as decided by the decision maker. Terms might, for instance, include that the foster carer may care only for a specific child, or for children of certain ages, or a certain number of children or take short or long-term placements. The fostering service should ensure that a carer's terms of approval reflect the type and number of children that the carer is happy and able to properly care for, and terms of approval should be kept under review to reflect any changes to these factors. This will ensure that a carer's terms of approval accurately reflect the children it is appropriate for them to care for.

Many foster carers are given broad terms of approval that reflect the needs of children who the service feels they are suitable to foster, given that matching procedures will consider each potential placement. A foster carer may not be considered suitable to care for a child outside their current terms of approval.

Regulation 27(5)(b) & schedule 5

Standard 21.11

Foster carers' terms of approval should be included in the foster care agreement, which they must sign when they are approved. The agreement also sets out the obligations of the foster carer, the complaints procedure, the support and training to be offered, and arrangements for review of approval.

Regulation 28

If a fostering service wishes to change a foster carer's terms of approval, it must carry out a review of the suitability of the foster carer and their household to continue to foster and of the appropriateness of their terms of approval, as described in the next section. The regulations do not make provision for changing approval terms on a temporary basis or without a review, or for reviewing terms of approval in isolation.

A foster carer is not allowed to foster more than three children unless the children are all siblings to each other or the foster carer is exempted from the 'usual fostering limit' of three by the local authority **in whose area they live**. Otherwise the foster carer will be regarded as running a children's home and need to register with Ofsted.

Reviewing approval

Regulation 28

Every foster carer's approval must be reviewed within a year of approval and then whenever the fostering service considers this necessary, but there must never be more than a year between reviews. The review must consider whether the foster carer and their household remain suitable to continue to foster and if the terms of approval are still appropriate. The review must consider all the information felt necessary to make this judgment, but as a minimum has to take into account the views of:

- the foster carer
- children in placement, if they are able to contribute
- any social worker responsible for a child in placement during the last year.

It is good practice to hold a meeting with the foster carer to consider all this information, and for this to be chaired independently. Reviews provide an opportunity to check if there have been any relevant changes since the last review, including any changes to the household that may need to be further considered. The foster carer's learning and development needs should be reviewed, as well as the effect of any support which has been provided and whether any additional support is required. However, these matters should be addressed when they arise and not just saved until the next review.

Standards 13.8 & 13.9

A review report must be written, and if this is the first review after approval it must be considered by the fostering panel. There is no legal requirement for subsequent reviews to be considered by the panel but fostering services may feel this to be helpful, particularly when they are considering changing the carer's terms of approval. The decision maker should consider the review report, and the recommendation (if any) of the fostering panel, and make their decision or qualifying determination as appropriate.

If having considered the review report the decision maker feels it appropriate to change the foster carer's terms of approval, a qualifying determination must be issued giving the foster carer 28 days to make representation or to apply to the IRM. However, the revised regulations permit the decision maker to change a foster carer's terms of approval without the need to first issue a qualifying determination (and therefore to wait for the 28 day response period) in circumstances when:

- a review of the foster carer's approval and terms has taken place in accordance with the regulations; and
- the fostering service provides the foster carer with a written statement setting out whether they consider the foster carer's household, including any children placed, to have additional support needs as a result of the proposed change, and if so what these needs are and how they will be met; and
- the foster carer agrees in writing to the change of terms of approval.

The decision making process following the qualifying determination is shown in the flow chart on page 58.

Ending approval

Regulation 28

A foster carer can at any time give written notice that they wish to resign, in which case their approval is terminated 28 days after the fostering service receives the notice. The decision maker does not, in any circumstances, have the power to decline a resignation, as this takes effect automatically after 28 days. Neither do the regulations permit a foster carer to withdraw their resignation once submitted in writing. Once a foster carer has resigned the fostering service has no responsibility to confirm this through panel, although it is good practice to notify the panel to inform its monitoring role. The fostering service should collate any final information on file to inform any future reference or consideration of the person's suitability to be a foster carer.

If a fostering service feels that a foster carer might no longer be suitable to remain approved, they should undertake a review, as described earlier in this section. Given the seriousness of the circumstances it will usually be appropriate for the fostering panel to consider the review report, even when this is not required by the regulations. If, taking into account any panel recommendation, the decision maker feels that the carer's approval should be terminated, then a qualifying determination must be issued and the subsequent decision making process will be determined by the response of the foster carer (as illustrated in the flow chart on page 58).

Things to think about: approval and review of foster carers

Fostering services

	yes	no
Does the fostering service make clear its criteria for being assessed as a foster carer?		
Is the assessment process made clear to applicants?		
Is a checklist used during assessments to distinguish between stage 1 and stage 2 information?		
Are reviews of foster carers sufficiently thorough to satisfy the fostering service about their ongoing suitability?		
Are areas of concern or support needs addressed as they arise, as well as at reviews?		
Are panel recommendations about approval made within eight months of application?		
Are all reviews of approval submitted to the decision maker, including any which recommend no change to approval details?		
Does the decision maker record clear reasons for decisions made?		
Is the decision maker a social worker with three years post-qualifying experience in child care social work, with knowledge of child care law and practice?		

15) Temporary approval of a connected person as a foster carer

Care Planning Placement and Case Review (England) Regulations 2010, regulations 24 & 25; Guidance 5.54 – 5.58; Family and Friends Care: Statutory Guidance for Local Authorities 5.3 - 5.13

Who is a 'connected person'?

Children Act 1989 s.105

A 'connected person' to a looked after child is a relative, friend or other person who has a connection with them. Relative means only a grandparent, brother, sister, uncle or aunt (either of full blood or half blood or by marriage or civil partnership) or a step-parent. A connected person could also be somebody with a professional relationship with the child, such as a childminder.

Granting temporary approval

Local authorities (but not IFPs) have the power to grant a connected person temporary approval as a foster carer in order for an immediate placement to be made. They must be satisfied that the placement is the most appropriate way to safeguard and promote a particular child's welfare and that the placement cannot wait until a full foster carer assessment can be completed. The statutory guidance explains that these powers are intended to be used exceptionally, in unforeseen circumstances. If there is no intention to undertake a full foster carer assessment, it will not be appropriate to grant temporary approval.

Children Act 1989 Guidance and Regulations Volume 2: Care Planning Placement and Case Review 3.85

In order to grant the temporary approval the authority must assess the suitability of the connected person to care for the child, including the suitability of their accommodation and of all members of the household over 18. The social worker must visit the home, and collect as much of the information listed in Schedule 4 to the Care Planning Placement and Case Review (England) Regulations 2010 as is possible in the circumstances. In particular, the assessment must consider the quality of any existing relationship between the child and the connected person. Discussions should take place about any criminal record, although it is not a requirement that a CRB disclosure should be received prior to temporary approval being granted. Other informal checks might be felt appropriate at this stage.

Ideally, the assessment at this stage will be carried out jointly by the child's social worker and a social worker from the fostering service, so that the child's needs can be considered alongside the responsibilities of being a foster carer. Local authorities need to nominate a member of staff with the authority to grant temporary approvals. Good practice suggests that this role should be given to the usual decision maker of the fostering service.

Standard 30.14

Temporary approval as a foster carer must be granted before the child is placed. Once temporary approval as a foster carer has been given under the care planning regulations, a full assessment under the fostering regulations should be started. To enable this, temporary approval may be granted for up to 16 weeks. In exceptional circumstances – if the full assessment takes longer than anticipated –the nominated officer can extend temporary approval for a further eight weeks, but must first seek a view from the fostering panel and inform the IRO. Only one extension of eight weeks can be granted. However, if a full assessment has been completed but the connected person has not been approved and has applied to the Independent Review Mechanism for a review, temporary approval can be extended until the outcome of the review is known.

If approval as a foster carer under the fostering regulations has not been completed within these timescales, temporary approval will end and the social worker must arrange a new placement for the child.

The following table suggests how responsibilities might be allocated in relation to temporary approval of a connected person as a foster carer.

Temporary approval of a connected person as a foster carer

Action	Suggested responsibility
Assess whether the placement is the best way to promote and safeguard the child's welfare	Child's social worker with supervising social worker
Present the assessment to the nominated officer	Child's social worker with supervising social worker

Temporary approval of a connected person as a foster carer *contd*

Action	Suggested responsibility
Grant temporary approval as a foster carer and set terms – eg name of child, duration	Local authority fostering service decision maker
Ensure the foster carer has all the information they need, including the care plan	Child's social worker
Prepare a placement plan	Child's social worker with foster carer and supervising social worker
Visit the child in placement	Child's social worker at least weekly until first review and then at least four weekly
Undertake full assessment	Supervising social worker with child's social worker
Supervise and support the foster carer as for all other foster carers	Supervising social worker
Arrange payments to the foster carer as for all other foster carers	Supervising social worker
Consider extension of temporary approval	Supervising social worker with child's social worker to report to fostering panel. Foster carers may attend panel.
Grant extension of temporary approval (once only)	Local authority nominated officer

Meaning of temporary approval

Care Planning Placement and Case Review (England) Regulations 2010 regulation 28(4)

Anyone who is temporarily approved as a foster carer under these arrangements is a foster carer in every respect other than the temporary nature of their approval. The foster carer must sign a foster carer agreement, and a care plan including a placement plan is required. The foster carer is entitled to the same support as all other foster carers, including training, practical support and allowances and fees according to the criteria set by the fostering service. The child's social worker is required to visit more frequently than for other foster placements. (See table on page 26).

Things to think about:
temporary approval of a connected person

Decision makers

Is the placement the most appropriate way to safeguard and promote the child's welfare in accordance with their care plan?

Can the placement await a full foster carer assessment under the Fostering Services (England) Regulations 2011?

Is the child's social worker jointly involved with the fostering service in assessing the person's suitability for temporary approval?

Is there any reason to think that the connected person might not be approved as a foster carer following a full assessment?

Has the quality of the child's relationship with the connected person been considered?

Has the social worker visited the home, and is the accommodation suitable?

Have all adult members of the household declared any criminal convictions and supplied information to enable DBS checks to be undertaken?

Has as much as possible of the information in Schedule 4 of the Care Planning Placement and Case Review (England) Regulations 2010 been considered?

Does the connected person understand the meaning of becoming a foster carer, and are they willing to sign a foster carer agreement?

Standard 30; Family and Friends Care: Statutory Guidance for Local Authorities, chapter 5

16) Family and friends foster carers

Policy requirement

Family and Friends Care: Statutory Guidance for Local Authorities, 4.2

Every local authority has to publish a family and friends care policy, explaining the way in which it supports family and friends carers. The policy must include information about family and friends foster care. The statement of purpose for the local authority fostering service must also include information relating to family and friends foster carers.

A 'connected person' who is approved as a foster carer for a particular child, including on a temporary basis, is usually known as a 'family and friends foster carer'.

The assessment

Even if they are initially approved on a temporary basis, family members, friends and other connected people must have a full assessment under the fostering regulations to continue to care for a child who is looked after by the local authority. The requirements of stages one and two apply as for all other fostering assessments. The NMS apply as they do to all fostering situations, and standard 30 specifically addresses family and friends foster carers.

The Fostering Network has produced *Family and Friends Foster Carers assessment materials*

Everything written in section 14 of this guide about approval and review of foster carers applies equally to family and friends foster carers, but there are important things which must be particularly considered during the assessment. The main points are briefly summarised here but they are explained in more detail in chapter 5 of *Family and Friends Care: Statutory Guidance for Local Authorities*.

Particular factors to consider

Placements with relatives and friends can often give a child more continuity than through moving to previously unknown foster carers, and this helps children to keep a sense of identity and belonging. However, relationships between parents and foster carers who are family members or friends can be complicated and so managing contact can be particularly difficult. The assessment should consider the carer's ability to manage the contact arrangements included in the care plan.

Family and friends foster carers are often motivated by family loyalty and commitment to the child and may be responding in an emergency, without an opportunity to consider the options and to plan ahead for the impact it will have upon them and their family. This may sometimes cause significant tensions within the family and so the assessment process may be particularly difficult for them and needs to be undertaken with sensitivity, particularly as there may be time constraints. It also provides an opportunity for families to fully think through all the implications of their decision.

Also, family and friends carers are often deeply affected personally by the events which have led to the child living away from their parents. They may be dealing with factors such as the death of their own child or the drug addiction of a sibling, which in other circumstances would probably make an assessment inappropriate at that time.

Lack of sufficient accommodation can also be a source of particular pressure, and must be seen as one part of the total assessment of suitability, to be balanced against other factors. For instance, a child who would be unhappy to share a bedroom with a child unknown to them may not mind sharing with another child who is a relative and who they know well. Relatives sometimes live a long way from the child's family home, and the requirement to place a child or young person near their home has to be balanced against other competing needs. Familiar surroundings may be less important than the ability to reinforce family ties but all relevant factors, including the wishes and feelings of the child and parents, must be taken into account in making the placement decision.

The health of the carers is also an important factor to consider in deciding whether a relative or friend is suitable to be approved as a foster carer, but again it should not be seen in isolation.

The carer's capacity to provide the necessary level of parenting to meet the child's particular needs is also important. The child's care plan will identify their developmental needs, and the carer's parenting capacity should be assessed in relation to those. The circumstances of the child's own parents may also have an impact on the capacity of the family member or friend to provide adequate care.

Regulation 26(8)

Providing the local authority is satisfied that the child's welfare requires it, a fostering service can (but does not have to) consider the approval of a foster carer for a particular child, even though the person would otherwise have been debarred because of a criminal conviction, if either the person wishing to become a foster carer or a member of their household is related to the child to be placed.

Support

As a result of their having an existing relationship with the child, family and friends foster carers are at risk of receiving insufficient support to help them to care for the child. Fostering services must ensure that family and friends foster carers are properly supported, and sometimes this will mean delivering support in a different way which takes account of the particular circumstances.

Things to think about: family and friends foster carers

Fostering services and children's social workers

When considering approval, is the carer's capacity to meet the child's needs, wishes and feelings taken into account?
Does the local authority work closely with other services to support the carer to care for the child?
Does the assessment take account of the likely length of the placement, the child's age, the wishes and feelings and any concerns of the child and, if appropriate, the capacity of the wider family to contribute to long term care?
Is it made clear to applicants what is expected of them and how they will be assessed, the criteria used and support to be offered?
Do social workers receive training about the particular needs of family and friends foster carers?
Where family and friends are temporarily approved under care planning regulations, is a full assessment under the fostering regulations always completed within statutory timescales?

Family and friends foster carers	yes	no
Are you given support, if necessary, to manage contact arrangements?		
Is the policy for financial support clear and fair?		
Are you able to access general foster carer training, and is there also specific training relevant to your particular needs?		
Can you attend relevant support groups?		

17) Moving to a new fostering service

Regulation 27(1) Assessment and Approval of Foster Carers: Amendments to the Children Act 1989 Guidance and Regulations July 2013

The Fostering Network has published a transfer protocol to guide this process. It can be downloaded from **www.fostering.net**

A foster carer cannot be approved by more than one fostering service at the same time. If a foster carer wishes to move to a different fostering service while a child remains placed with them, the relevant fostering services, local authorities and the foster carer will need to liaise to agree how this can best be achieved, taking account of the timescales and other requirements of the regulations and NMS. Approval by the existing service must be terminated (which will usually be by way of the foster carer's resignation) before a decision by the new service to grant approval can be implemented.

If an applicant has been approved previously, or is currently approved, as a foster carer or prospective adopter then with the applicant's permission the service which is undertaking the new assessment can request access to the records of that other fostering service or adoption agency. This is to inform their assessment at stage one. The statutory guidance on assessment and approval of foster carers clearly explains what information should be shared.

Regulation 26(1)(d)]

Regulation 32(6); Standard 26.9

The information has to be made available to another fostering service or an adoption agency within 15 working days of the request, and this may require seeking the permission of third parties to share their personal information and/or redaction of records. The statutory guidance references further sources of information including a guide on how to share information securely. It also makes clear that any information which has given cause for concern about a foster carer's conduct or suitability to foster should be shared even if consent to do so has been refused. Under the Data Protection Act 1998 an individual has subject access rights to information held about them, and can obtain copies of their records to inform a new assessment.

Standard 20.11

Details of the training and development undertaken by a foster carer should be made available to any new fostering service, and foster carers can take their training and development portfolio with them.

If an independent fostering provider ceases to operate and does not make arrangements with another provider to take over its service, each of its approved foster carers will, by default, become foster carers for the local authority in whose area they live and that local authority must decide within 16 weeks whether or not to re-approve them after making its own assessment. If it is not practical to complete the re-approval within 16 weeks the period can be extended to enable the process to be completed.

Regulations 33-34; Guidance 5.74

Things to think about: moving to a new fostering service

Fostering services

	yes	no
If a foster carer wants to move to a new service, do the parties involved work together to enable this while keeping a focus on the best interests of any child in placement?		
Is The Fostering Network transfer protocol followed when foster carers wish to move to another service?		
Do foster carers retain their training and development portfolio when they move to a new fostering service?		
Does the previous fostering service provide information to the new service within 15 days of a written request?		

Regulations 22 & 30-32 & schedules 2 and 3; Standard 26; Guidance 5.75-5.79

18) Keeping records

Every fostering service has to have a clear policy to enable foster carers and staff to keep clear records about children in placement, and the work undertaken by foster carers. Information recorded should be non-stigmatising and distinguish between fact and opinion, and children should know how to access records kept about them and be encouraged to do so. All records must be kept confidentially.

Fostering services are required to keep certain records. Records in relation to each foster carer, including their assessment, approval and details of children placed with them, must be kept for at least 10 years after the carer's approval has ended. Records relating to people who do not go on to be approved as foster carers must be kept for at least three years. Every service must also keep a register of foster carers, and of children placed with foster carers. Information about children placed has to be kept for 15 years.

Regulation 36(1) & schedule 7; Standards 25 & 29; Guidance 4.8

Managers of fostering services are required to monitor the records kept to make sure that policies are adhered to and to identify any concerns. An IFP has to notify certain events to Ofsted, and the manager of a local authority fostering service should also use this information about the quality of care provided by the service to drive service improvements.

Things to think about: keeping records

Fostering services

Is there a clear policy about keeping records, including the child's file, foster carer files and fostering service records?

Do fostering households, staff and others understand what records are kept, and are there systems for monitoring quality?

Are records kept in a way which facilitates sharing of information within 15 working days is required?

Are children encouraged to read their files?

Are all records non-stigmatising, do they distinguish between fact and opinion, and are they kept confidentially?

19) Fostering for adoption

Care Planning, Placement and Case Review and Fostering Services (Miscellaneous Amendments) Regulations 2013 Early permanence placements and approval of prospective adopters as foster carers: Statutory guidance for local authorities and adoption agencies

Sometimes the risk of a looked after child having placement moves can be reduced by placing them with foster carers who will become their adopters if a placement order is made subsequently allowing the placement to become one for adoption. This practice is known as fostering for adoption and is most likely to arise for very young children where there are strong indications that adoption is likely to be the outcome. Such placements are fostering placements, not placements for adoption.

The care planning regulations have been amended to permit a person, who has been approved as a prospective adopter, to be temporarily approved by a looked after child's responsible local authority as the foster carer for that child, without having to be approved as a foster carer under the fostering regulations. The temporary approval relates specifically to a named child (or children). An assessment under the fostering regulations is not required as the carer will already have been assessed and approved as a prospective adopter. There is an additional requirement to assess their suitability to care for the specific child as a foster carer but there are no stipulations regarding the content of that assessment.

The circumstances in which temporary approval as a foster carer can be granted, and in which it is terminated, are set out in regulation 25A of the revised care planning regulations and the related statutory guidance.

A temporarily approved foster carer is a foster carer with the same rights and responsibilities as other foster carers, since the definition of foster parent in the fostering regulations has been amended to include those with temporary approval under the new care planning regulation 25A. Such foster carers need to sign a foster care agreement and to be supervised, supported and paid in the same way as other foster carers, and to understand the legal framework and standards relating to foster care.

Things to think about: keeping records

Fostering services

Is there a local policy regarding the assessment and approval of prospective adopters as temporary foster carers?

How are the foster carers supported and supervised?

Do the prospective adopters understand all the responsibilities of fostering a child?

Where to go for help

The Fostering Network delivers confidential advice lines for foster carers and provides independent, impartial advice about fostering issues.

Member helpline
the foster carers' adviceline
t 020 7401 9582
10am-3pm, Monday-Friday
e info@fostering.net

There is a lot of useful information available on The Fostering Network's website **www.fostering.net**

The Fostering Network's foster carer membership provides foster carers with access to a range of expert advice, information and support services including advice lines, online resources and essentially, legal protection insurance in the case of an allegation. Find out more about our foster carer membership online at **www.fostering.net/membership** or **e** info@fostering.net

Independent support for foster carers
The Fostering Network's advice and mediation service provides independent advice and mediation to foster carers, particularly during the investigation of allegations. If you are a foster carer, ask your fostering service if they commission the service from The Fostering Network. If you are a fostering service that doesn't yet offer this crucial support service for your foster carers, contact our independent support services manager for more information at **e** info@fostering.net

Glossary

Allegation – an accusation of physical, emotional or sexual abuse, or serious neglect, of a child or young person by a foster carer or other member of the foster family.

Allowance – payment given to foster carers to cover the cost of the child's care including food, clothing, transport and pocket money.

Assessment – this is the process undertaken to ensure that a person is suitable to become a foster carer. The assessment process includes interviews, training, references and other checks.

Care plan – every looked after child should have a care plan which will include details of their needs and how these will be met, and contain information about their placement and the longer-term planning for their care.

Child's social worker – this is a social worker who is provided by the responsible authority to work with a child and to plan for their care. They are also responsible for meeting with the child to ensure that the child's needs are being met.

Connected person – a connected person is a family member (whether by birth or marriage/civil partnership), friend of, or other person who is known to, the child. They can be child minders, teachers, youth workers or others working in a professional capacity with the child.

Contact – the process whereby children stay in touch with people who are important to them, including relatives such as parents and grandparents as well as others, such as former foster carers.

DBS check – enquiry made of the Disclosure and Barring Service to check if a person has an existing criminal record in the UK. Previously known as CRB check.

Delegated authority – this is where the responsibility for making day-to-day decisions about a child has been passed to the foster carer. This can include decisions around activities, haircuts and overnight stays.

Family and friends foster care – where a child was previously known to their foster carer and their foster carer was approved to look after them, this is known as family and friends foster care. More comprehensive guidance on family and friends foster care is given in *Family and Friends Care: statutory guidance for local authorities*

Fee – this is a payment made to a foster carer for their work as a foster carer.

Fostering panel – the panel is a group of appointed people who make recommendations on the approval of prospective foster carers and changes to the approval of existing foster carers. Details of who has to sit on this panel are covered in Regulation 23.

Fostering service decision maker – this is a senior person within the fostering service who makes a final decision on the recommendations from the fostering panel (see above). The qualifications required for this role are explained in National Minimum Standard 23.

IFP – an IFP (Independent Fostering Provider) is an organisation that places children into foster placements on behalf of the local authority.

Independent Review Mechanism (IRM) – the IRM reviews, on behalf of the secretary of state, qualifying determinations issued by fostering services.

Independent Reviewing Officer (IRO) – the IRO is a social worker who takes part in the reviews for children in care. They chair the review and monitor implementation of the care plan, as well as ensuring that the child's voice is heard and that their wishes are taken into account.

Local authority – the local council that has responsibility for children's services, including provision for looked after children.

National Minimum Standards – these describe the absolute minimum standard of service expected by the government, which fostering services must provide. They are used during inspections to check the regulations are being met.

Ofsted – the Office for Standards in Education, Children's Services and Skills (Ofsted) is the government body responsible for inspecting fostering services in England. All independent fostering providers have to be registered with Ofsted.

Pathway plan – the pathway plan is completed as part of the leaving care process for each young person and includes any actions that have to be carried out by the responsible authority, foster carer, the young person themselves and any others involved.

Personal Education Plan (PEP) – the PEP is part of the child's care plan and gives information about the arrangements that have been made for their educational and/or training needs by the responsible authority.

Placement plan – the placement plan forms part of the child's overall care plan and lays out how the placement will meet the particular child's needs.

Qualifying determination – this is where a fostering service is considering to not approve a prospective foster carer, wishes to change the terms of approval of an existing foster carer or feels a foster carer is no longer suitable to foster. In the case of receiving a qualifying determination that they don't agree with, prospective and existing foster carers can make representations to the fostering service or they can ask the IRM to review the situation. However, they cannot do both.

Regulations – these outline the legal requirements for foster care and all fostering services must comply with them. Failure to do so is a breach of the law.

Responsible authority - this is the authority that has responsibility for ensuring that the child is appropriately looked after while in its care.

Short breaks – these are a series of placements made for a limited amount of time where the child then returns to their parents. This does not include children who are subject to a care order.

Special Guardianship – when the court makes a Special Guardianship order it gives parental responsibility to the special guardian, which they share with anyone else who has this. The order lasts until the child is 18, unless the court discharges it earlier.

Statement of purpose – required by law under the Fostering Services (England) Regulations 2011, the statement of purpose must include the aims and objectives of the fostering service as well as the services and facilities that they offer. The statement of purpose has to be placed on the fostering service's website if they have one.

Staying Put – arrangement whereby a fostered young person remains living with their foster carer when they turn 18.

Usual fostering limit – under the Children Act 1989 Schedule 7, the number of children fostered by a foster carer is limited (the usual fostering limit). The usual fostering limit is three children unless the children are all siblings although exemptions can be granted.

Further resources from The Fostering Network

order online from **www.fosteringresources.co.uk**

All You Need to Know: a Foster Care Handbook for Supervising Social Workers (England)
This detailed handbook explains in clear, easy-to-read terms the complex legal requirements which govern fostering services and offers practical advice about how to meet these. It is an invaluable source of information not just for supervising social workers but for everyone who plays a part in delivering foster care services.

All You Need to Know: Planning for Looked After Children – a handbook for children's social workers (England)
A comprehensive handbook to help children's social workers understand what they need to do to meet the legal requirements that govern their work with looked after children. Updated to take account of legislative changes, it follows the child's journey through care planning, placement, case review and transition to adulthood, and includes practical guidance on working effectively with foster carers and staff in fostering services and children's homes.

All You Need to Know: Family and Friends Foster Care – a handbook for foster carers (England)
This guide has been specially written for everyone who is thinking about becoming a family and friends foster carer, those who are family and friends foster carers already and social workers and others who work with these carers. It includes an up-to-date explanation of the legal framework that governs fostering services and family and friends foster care.

Signposts in Fostering
A series of information booklets giving both new and experienced foster carers information in a simple and accessible format.

Allegations
Record Keeping
Benefits
Income Tax and National Insurance
Welcoming the Fostered Child
Working with Social Workers

Pathways Through Fostering

A series of practical guides focusing on dealing with day-to-day challenges, rather than complicated theory. Packed with helpful guidance and case studies to help foster carers enhance knowledge and develop skills.

Attachment

Behaviour

Contact

Education

Health

Safer Caring: a new approach

Fostering in a Digital World provides foster carers and other professionals with essential information and tools to enable fostered children to benefit from using laptops, gaming consoles, tablets and mobile phones, while managing risk sensibly and effectively.

The Skills to Foster (third edition) is for foster carers across the UK and is mapped to *The Training Support and Development Standards*, which are a mandatory requirement for foster carers in England. It provides a more flexible resource that supports all foster carers taking on different types of placements, including family and friends foster carers.

Prepared to Care: a resource book for family and friends carers

Medical Treatment Authorisation Card

The Skills to Foster Assessment – applying to foster: an applicant's guide to the assessment process

The Skills to Foster Assessment – assessing foster carers: a social worker's guide

The Skills to Foster Assessment – family and friends

The Skills to Foster Assessment – licence

Further resources from The Fostering Network *contd*

Resources for children and young people

Living in Foster Care: a guide for children

Living in Foster Care: a guide for young people

My Family Fosters

Preparation for Adult Life

Free resources from The Fostering Network

download from **www.fostering.net**

Heart of the Matter: resources on contact for foster carers and fostering services

Supporting Placement Planning: resources from The Fostering Network's delegated authority project

Growing Up in Our House: poetry and short stories by children and young people who live in foster families